ELITE UNIT INSIGNIA
OF THE VIETNAM WAR
An illustrated reference guide
for collectors

ELITE
UNIT INSIGNIA
OF THE VIETNAM WAR
An illustrated reference guide
for collectors

Leroy Thompson

ARMS AND ARMOUR PRESS
LONDON NEW YORK SYDNEY

ACKNOWLEDGEMENTS
I would like to thank the following collectors
who gave me assistance on this book: Harry Pugh, Hal Feldman,
Lou DiPonziano, Pete McDermott, Andy Paul and Ken Lewis.

First published in Great Britain
in 1986 by Arms and Armour Press Limited,
2–6 Hampstead High Street, London NW3 1QQ.

Distributed in the USA by Sterling Publishing Co. Inc.,
2 Park Avenue, New York, N.Y. 10016.

Distributed in Australia by
Capricorn Link (Australia) Pty. Ltd., P.O. Box 665,
Lane Cove, New South Wales 2066, Australia.

British Library Cataloguing in Publication Data:
Thompson, Leroy
Elite unit insignia of the Vietnam War:
an illustrated reference guide for collectors. –
(Illustrated reference guides for collectors)
1. United States. *Army, Special Forces –*
– Insignia –
History
I. Title II. Series
355.1′4 UC533
ISBN 0-85368-815-X

Designed by David Gibbons; edited by
Debbie Fox, typeset by Typesetters (Birmingham) Ltd;
printed and bound in Great Britain.

CONTENTS

INTRODUCTION

The diversity of units assigned to carry out special missions engendered a vast number of colorful and interesting insignia. Because it was so easy to go to a local tailor's shop and have insignia made up for a particular unit and because of the wide usage of unauthorized insignia, there were literally many hundreds of insignia worn by the various US and Vietnamese airborne, special forces, long range patrol, ranger, SEAL (Sea Air Land Team), or recon (Reconnaissance) troops. This book makes no claim to completeness, since there were so many insignia worn by so many units. An attempt has been made, however, to illustrate as many types of elite insignia as possible, so that the collector can recognize the style, construction, and heraldic themes of the insignia worn during the Vietnam conflict.

Most serious collectors of insignia of the Vietnam war want insignia actually made within the Republic of Vietnam during the conflict. In many cases this will mean hand-made insignia, or insignia produced on a single sewing machine in a small tailor's shop. In the case of some US insignia and some Vietnamese insignia, however, machine-made insignia produced in some quantity are also considered quite collectable. It should be pointed out as well that frequently US personnel, especially those of the Special Forces, would have insignia for their A-Team (Basic Special Forces operational unit) or Recon Team made up while on R&R (Rest and Recuperation) in Bangkok, Hong Kong, or elsewhere. If actually produced during the war for units serving in Vietnam, such insignia are normally considered as made 'in country'. For the most part in this work I have illustrated only insignia I am relatively confident has been made 'in country'. In a few cases, such as the SEAL breast badge (Item 5) and the Pararescue beret badge (Item 7) some of the DIs (Distinctive Insignias) Items 8–20, and the Special Forces items 55–8, I have chosen to illustrate insignia made in the USA but widely worn in Southeast Asia. However, locally produced examples of many of these items may also exist. In the case of DIs, for example, many were produced in Vietnam in what is called 'beer can' form, because of the thin, cheap metal used.

Because of the recent interest in the Vietnam war and the growth of collecting insignia of the war, fakes or reproduction insignia now abound. 'Buyer beware' definitely applies when buying insignia of the Vietnam War. One must be especially careful of the most highly collected insignia, such as the MACV/

SOG (Military Assistance Command Vietnam/Studies and Observation Group) recon team pocket patches, most of which were originally made in only limited quantity. These have been reproduced in machine-made versions, and some have been reproduced in hand-made versions. To aid the collector in spotting fakes, I have limited the number of insignia illustrated on a page, so that each can be shown in greater detail. Fortunately, many of the most desirable Vietnamese insignia were made in silk and, to the best of my knowledge, no one has found it worthwhile to fake these yet. These silk insignia are especially aesthetically pleasing and, for the time being, can normally be assumed to be authentic. Still, I advise novice collectors to study the texture of the insignia identified as silk in this work. Remember too that many insignia made in silk were printed on cloth as well.

A note on elite units in Vietnam is probably in order. Among US units, the 5th Special Forces Group (Airborne), the 173rd Airborne Brigade, 1st Cavalry Division (Airmobile), 82nd Airborne Division, and 101st Airborne Division were the five major 'elite' formations serving in Vietnam. To these larger units, however, must be added the long range patrol units that carried out reconnaissance missions in contested country and that later in the war were consolidated under the 75th Rangers. Other Rangers served as advisors to the Vietnamese Rangers. Some US airborne personnel were also advisors to the Viet airborne units; these and other paratroopers were often assigned directly to MACV. The 46th Special Forces Company (Airborne) in Thailand also played a key role during the war. Special Forces projects such as MACV/SOG, Projects Delta, Sigma, and Omega, and the Phoenix Program, also made use of a large number of 'green berets'. The US Navy's SEALs are often ranked as the toughest US personnel in Vietnam, although their numbers were limited. The USMC (United States Marine Corps) Recons and Air Force CCTs (Combat Control Teams), Pararescue, and Combat Security Police were also elite troops given special training and assigned special missions. 'Recondo' is another term often heard in conjunction with the Vietnam war. The Recondo – or Reconnaissance Commando – training center at Nha Trang turned out LRRPs (Long Range Reconnaissance Patrols) and others needing special deep penetration reconnaissance and raiding skills. The MACV/Recondo School pocket patch was one of the most prized awards in Vietnam.

Among the Vietnamese, there were both large and small elite units. The LLDB (Vietnamese Special Forces), the ARVN (Army of the Republic of Vietnam) Airborne Brigade – later a Division, the ARVN Rangers, and the Viet Marines, were all large elite units. Also important, however, were the Hac Baos (Black Panthers) of the 1st Infantry Division's Strike Company, the

LLDN (the Viet SEALs), and the PRUs (Provincial Reconnaissance Units). The 'prews' were, along with the ARVN Rangers, often rated the most effective indigenous troops. PRUs were often mercenaries, some of which were drawn from communist turncoats, but they were tough and well-motivated (sometimes by profit) and justly deserved their reputation. Noteworthy also are the Nungs and Montagnards trained by the US Special Forces as elite strike units. The MIKE (Mobile Strike) Forces, Mobile Guerrilla Forces, and the indigenous elements of MACV/SOG, or other recon units, drew primarily from these two ethnic minorities.

Although not covered within this book, there are also elite insignia of the Cambodian, South Korean, Thai, and Laotian armies during the Vietnam conflict. The Cambodians especially were often trained by members of the US Special Forces assigned to FANK (Forces Armee National Khymer) and offer an interesting adjunct to a collection of US and Vietnamese elite insignia. Authentic Cambodian and Laotian elite insignia from the war are, however, quite scarce.

As with so many collectables, the interest in Vietnam insignia is growing, but the number of authentic insignia of the war remains finite. In some ways the stigma attached to the war and its veterans caused many veterans to burn, or otherwise destroy, uniforms and insignia, rather than retain them – another reason for their scarcity. Fortunately for the collector, most members of elite units took pride in their accomplishment of having served with an airborne, ranger, or special forces unit and, as a result, retained examples of their insignia. I emphasize once again, however, that authentic insignia of the Vietnam war, especially locally-made US insignia, must be viewed very carefully before investing the very substantial sums now being asked for them. Whenever possible, purchases should be made from a veteran who actually brought back the insignia, or from a dealer with a reputation for honesty and expertise.

Though by no means complete, this reference guide will, I hope, prove useful to both novice and veteran collectors of insignia of the Vietnam war. Many of the insignia illustrated in this book, which will find their way into collections, were not authorized and were often not worn openly. Many of the SOG insignia, for example, were sewn inside berets. In many ways I believe this 'clandestine' nature of some of the insignia is appealing, since it was a subtle way for the men wearing unobtrusive insignia to say that they were proud of their unit, their country, and the fact that they were doing a dirty job professionally.

PRICE GUIDE

Item	Rated	$ value	£ value
1.	C	$2.50–$5	£2–£4
2.	FS	$4–$8	£3–£6
3.	VR	$25–$50	£20–£40
4.	VU	$100–$200	£75–£100
5.	FS	$5–$10	£4–£8
6.	C	$3–$5	£2–£4
7.	FS	$5–$10	£4–£8

8–20. *US-made 'beer can' and US-made distinctive insignias for elite units:*

Item	Rated	$ value	£ value
8.	VR	$15–$25	£10–£20
9.	C	$2.50–$5	£2–£4
10.	C	$2.50–$5	£2–£4
11.	C	$2.50–$5	£2–£4
12.	C	$2.50–$5	£2–£4
13.	C	$2.50–$5	£2–£4
14.	C	$2.50–$5	£2–£4
15.	C	$2.50–$5	£2–£4
16.	C	$2.50–$5	£2–£4
17.	C	$2.50–$5	£2–£4
18.	C	$2.50–$5	£2–£4
19.	C	$2.50–$5	£2–£4
20.	C	$2.50–$5	£2–4

21–8. *'In-country' hand-made or locally-made para ovals:*

Item	Rated	$ value	£ value
21.	VR	$10–$25	£10–£20
22.	VR	$10–$25	£10–£20
23.	VR	$10–$25	£10–£20
24.	VR	$10–$25	£10–£20
25.	VR	$10–$25	£10–£20
26.	VR	$10–$25	£10–£20
27.	VR	$10–$25	£10–£20

28–30. *Locally-made sniper insignia:*

Item	Rated	$ value	£ value
28.	VR	$25–$50	£20–£40
29.	VR	$25–$50	£20–£40
30.	VR	$25–$50	£20–£40

31–5. *Locally-made 1st Air Cavalary:*

Item	Rated	$ value	£ value
31.	VR	$20–$50	£20–£40
32.	VR	$20–$50	£20–£40
33.	VR	$20–$50	£20–£40
34.	VR	$20–$50	£20–£40
35.	VR	$20–$50	£20–£40
36.	R	$15	£10
37.	R	$15	£10
38.	R	$15	£10
39.	R	$15	£10
40.	VR	$15	£12
41.	VR	$15	£12
42.	R	$15	£10
43.	R	$15	£10
44.	VR	$15	£12

Item	Rated	$ value	£ value
45.	R	$15	£10
46.	VR	$15	£12
47.	VR	$15	£12

48–52. *Locally-made LRRP or Recon insignia:*

Item	Rated	$ value	£ value
48.	VR	$15–$50	£10–£35
49.	VR	$15–$50	£10–£35
50.	VR	$15–$50	£10–£35
51.	VR	$15–$50	£10–£30
52.	R	$15–$50	£10–£30
53.	R	$15	£12
54.	R	$15–$50	£12–£25

55–8. *US-made Special Forces:*

Item	Rated	$ value	£ value
55.	C	$2.50–$5	£2–£4
56.	C	$2.50–$5	£2–£4
57.	C	$2.50–$5	£2–£4
58.	C	$2.50–$5	£2–£4

59–64. *Locally-made Special Forces beret flashes:*

Item	Rated	$ value	£ value
59.	VR	$15–$35	£10–£25
60.	VR	$15–$35	£10–£25
61.	R	$15–$35	£10–£25
62.	VR	$15–$35	£10–£25
63.	VR	$15–$35	£10–£25
64.	VR	$15–$35	£10–£25
65.	VR	$15–$35	£10–£25
66.	VR	$50–$75	£40–£60
67.	R	$35–$50	£20–£35

68–124. *Hand-made or locally-tailor-shop-made MACV or Project Delta, Sigma, Omega, etc. insignia:*

Item	Rated	$ value	£ value
68.	VR	$40–$60	£30–£40
69.	VR	$50–$100	£40–£80
70.	VR	$35–$70	£25–£50
71.	VR	$35–$70	£25–£50
72.	VR	$35–$70	£25–£50
73.	VR	$35–$70	£25–£50
74.	VR	$35–$70	£25–£50
75.	VR	$35–$70	£25–£50
76.	VR	$35–$70	£25–£50
77.	VR	$35–$70	£25–£50
78.	VR	$35–$70	£25–£50
79.	VR	$35–$70	£25–£50
80.	VR	$35–$70	£25–£50
81.	VR	$35–$70	£25–£50
82.	VR	$35–$70	£25–£50
83.	VR	$35–$70	£25–£50
84.	VR	$35–$70	£25–£50
85.	VR	$35–$70	£25–£50
86.	VR	$35–$70	£25–£50

Item	Rated	$ value	£ value
87.	VR	$35–$70	£25–£50
88.	VR	$35–$70	£25–£50
89.	VR	$35–$70	£25–£50
90.	VR	$35–$70	£25–£50
91.	VR	$35–$70	£25–£50
92.	VR	$35–$70	£25–£50
93.	VR	$35–$70	£25–£50
94.	VR	$35–$70	£25–£50
95.	VR	$35–$70	£25–£50
96.	VR	$35–$70	£25–£50
97.	VR	$35–$70	£25–£50
98.	VR	$35–$70	£25–£50
99.	VR	$35–$70	£25–£50
100.	VR	$35–$70	£25–£50
101.	VR	$35–$70	£25–£50
102.	VR	$50–$100	£35–£70
103.	VR	$35–$70	£25–£50
104.	VR	$35–$70	£25–£50
105.	VR	$35–$70	£25–£50
106.	VR	$35–$70	£25–£50
107.	VR	$35–$70	£25–£50
108.	VR	$35–$70	£25–£50
109.	VR	$35–$70	£35–£70
110.	VR	$50–$100	£35–£70
111.	VR	$35–$70	£25–£50
112.	VR	$35–$70	£25–£50
113.	VR	$35–$70	£25–£50
114.	VR	$35–$70	£25–£50
115.	VR	$35–$70	£25–£50
116.	VR	$35–$70	£25–£50
117.	VR	$35–$70	£25–£50
118.	VR	$35–$70	£25–£50
119.	R	$35–$70	£20–£40
120.	VR	$35–$70	£25–£50
121.	VR	$35–$70	£25–£50
122.	VR	$50–$100	£35–£70
123.	VU	$50–$100	£35–£70
124.	VU	$100–$150	£75–£125
125.	VR	$10–$15	£7.50–£12.50
126.	VU	$35–$50	£20–£40
127.	VU	$35–$50	£20–£40
128.	VU	$35–$75	£25–£50
129.	VU	$35–$75	£25–£50
130.	VR	$35–$75	£20–£40
131.	VR	$35–$75	£20–£40
132.	VR	$10–$15	£7.50–£12.50
133.	VR	$10–$15	£10–£12.50
134.	VU	$25–$35	£20–£30

135–7. Vietnam-made (in-country) para brevets – basic, senior, master, instructor, jump status etc:

Item	Rated	$ value	£ value
135.	R	$15–$35	£10–£20
136.	R	$15–$35	£10–£20
137.	R	$15–$35	£10–£20

138–40. Locally-made 'beer can' DIs for Viet elite units

Item	Rated	$ value	£ value
138.	VR	$15–$35	£10–£20
139.	VR	$15–$35	£10–£20
140.	VR	$15–$35	£10–£20
141.	VR	$15–$35	£10–£20

(NB. Specially made ranger badges in gold and silver etc. may bring a much higher price.)

Item	Rated	$ value	£ value
142.	R	$10–$20	£5–£10
143.	R	$10–$20	£5–£10
144.	R	$10–$20	£5–£10
145.	VR	$20–$35	£10–£20

(NB. Quite scarce and often brings a premium as will some cloth versions of the LLDB wings.)

Item	Rated	$ value	£ value
146.	R	$10–$20	£5–£10
147.	R	$10–$20	£5–£10
148.	R	$10–$20	£5–£10
149.	R	$10–$20	£5–£10
150.	R	$10–$20	£5–£10
151.	R	$10–$20	£5–£10
152.	R	$10–$50	£5–£10
153.	R	$10–$50	£10–£15
154.	R	$10–$50	£5–£10
155.	R	$10–$50	£10–£15
156.	R	$10–$50	£5–£10
157.	R	$10–$50	£10–£15
158.	R	$10–$50	£10–£15
159.	R	$10–$50	£10–£15
160.	R	$10–$50	£10–£15
161.	VR	$10–$25	£7.50–£15
162.	VR	$10–$25	£7.50–£15
163.	VR	$10–$25	£7.50–£15
164.	VR	$10–$25	£7.50–£15
165.	VR	$7.50–$15	£7.50–£15
166.	VR	$10–$25	£7.50–£15
167.	VR	$10–$25	£10–£20
168.	R	$10–$25	£7.50–£15
169.	R	$10–$25	£7.50–£15
170.	R	$10–$25	£7.50–£15
171.	R	$10–$25	£7.50–£15
172.	R	$10–$25	£10–£20
173.	R	$10–$25	£7.50–£15
174.	R	$10–$25	£10–£15
175.	R	$10–$25	£7.50–£15

176–96. MIKE Force and other US Special Forces trained reation forces:

Item	Rated	$ value	£ value
176.	VR	$12.50–$25	£10–£20
177.	R	$7.00–$20	£7.50–£15
178.	VR	$12.50–$50	£10–£20
179.	VR	$12.50–$50	£10–£20
180.	VR	$12.50–$50	£10–£20
181.	R	$7.50–$20	£7.50–£15
182.	R	$7.50–$20	£7.50–£15
183.	R	$7.50–$20	£7.50–£15
184.	VR	$12.50–$50	£10–£20
185.	VR	$12.50–$50	£10–£20
186.	VR	$12.50–$50	£10–£20
187.	VR	$12.50–$50	£10–£20

Item	Rated	$ value	£ value
188.	VR	$12.50–$50	£10–£20
189.	VR	$12.50–$50	£10–£20
190.	R	$7.50–$20	£7.50–£15
191.	R	$12.50–$50	£10–£20
192.	R	$7.50–$20	£7.50–£15
193.	R	$7.00–$20	£7.50–£15
194.	R	$7.00–$20	£7.50–£15
195.	R	$7.50–$20	£7.50–£15
196.	VR	$12.50–$50	£10–£20

197–9. *ARVN Ranger arcs:*

Item	Rated	$ value	£ value
197.	R	$5–$10	£5–£10
198.	R	$5–$10	£5–£10
199.	R	$5–$10	£5–£10
200.	VR	$15–$35	£10–£20
201.	VR	$15–$35	£10–£20
202.	VR	$15–$35	£15–£25
203.	R	$15–$35	£10–£20

204–6. *Hac Bao insignia:*

Item	Rated	$ value	£ value
204.	R	$7.50–$20	£7.50–£15
205.	R	$7.50–$20	£7.50–£15
206.	R	$7.50–$20	£7.50–£15

207–14. *PRU insignia:*

Item	Rated	$ value	£ value
207.	VR	$20–$30	£15–£30
208.	VR	$20–$30	£15–£30
209.	VR	$20–$30	£15–£30
210.	VR	$20–$30	£15–£30
211.	R	$15–$25	£10–£15
212.	R	$15–$25	£10–£15
213.	R	$15–$25	£10–£15
214.	R	$15–$25	£10–£15
215.	R	$5–$10	£4–£8
216.	R	$15–$25	£10–£20

217–32. *ARVN airborne insignia:*

Item	Rated	$ value	£ value
217.	R	$12.50–$25	£10–£20
218.	R	$12.50–$25	£10–£20
219.	R	$12.50–$25	£10–£20
220.	R	$12.50–$25	£10–£20
221.	R	$12.50–$25	£10–£20
222.	R	$12.50–$25	£10–£20
223.	R	$12.50–$25	£10–£20
224.	R	$12.50–$25	£10–£20
225.	R	$12.50–$25	£10–£20
226.	R	$12.50–$25	£10–£20
227.	R	$12.50–$25	£10–£20
228.	R	$12.50–$25	£10–£20
229.	R	$12.50–$25	£10–£20
230.	VR	$20–$30	£15–£25
231.	VR	$20–$30	£15–£25
232.	R	$12.50–$25	£10–£20

233–42. *Viet Marine pocket or shoulder sleeve insignia:*

Item	Rated	$ value	£ value
233.	R	$12.50–$25	£10–£20
234.	R	$12.50–$25	£10–£20
235.	R	$12.50–$25	£10–£20
236.	R	$12.50–$25	£10–£20
237.	R	$12.50–$25	£10–£20
238.	R	$12.50–$25	£10–£20

Item	Rated	$ value	£ value
239.	R	$12.50–$25	£10–£20
240.	R	$12.50–$25	£10–£20
241.	R	$12.50–$25	£10–£20
242.	R	$12.50–$25	£10–£20
243.	R	$12.50–$25	£10–£20
244.	R	$15–$25	£15–£30

(NB. Full set of the different colors is worth $150 or more.)

Item	Rated	$ value	£ value
245.	VR	$15–$25	£15–£30

GLOSSARY AND
LIST OF ABBREVIATIONS

GLOSSARY

A-Team	Basic Special Forces operational unit
ABN	Airborne
ARVN	Army of the Republic of Vietnam
AVN	Aviation
Battn	Battalion
Cav	Cavalry
CCC	Command and Control Central
CCN	Command and Control North
CCT	Combat Control Team
CIDG	Civilian Irregular Defense Group
DI	Distinctive Insignia
Div	Division
FAC	Forward Area Cambodia
HALO	High Altitude Low Opening
Inf	Infantry
LLDN	Viet SEALs (frogmen)
LRRP	Long Range Reconnaissance Patrol
MACV	Military Assistance Command Vietnam
MIKE Forces	Mobile Strike Forces
PRU	Provincial Reconnaissance Unit
Psy Ops	Psychological Operations
R&R	Rest and Recuperation
Recon Team	Reconnaissance Team
SEAL	Sea Air Land Team
SOG	Studies Observations Group
SSI	Shoulder Sleeve Insignia
USMC	United States Marine Corps

ABBREVIATIONS USED IN THE PRICE GUIDE

C	Common items readily available.
FS	Fairly scarce items that are obtainable, but not without a degree of effort on the part of the collector.
R	Rare items that are obtainable, but require a lot of hard work to locate.
VR	Very rare items commanding top prices, or which become available only when splitting up a good-quality collection.
VU	Virtually unobtainable. Items so rare as to be considered non-existent.

ABBREVIATIONS USED IN THE CAPTION LIST

B	Bullion
HM	Hand-made
M	Metal
MM	Machine-made
P	Printed
SEA	Made in Southeast Asia
SW	Silk-woven
US	Made in USA

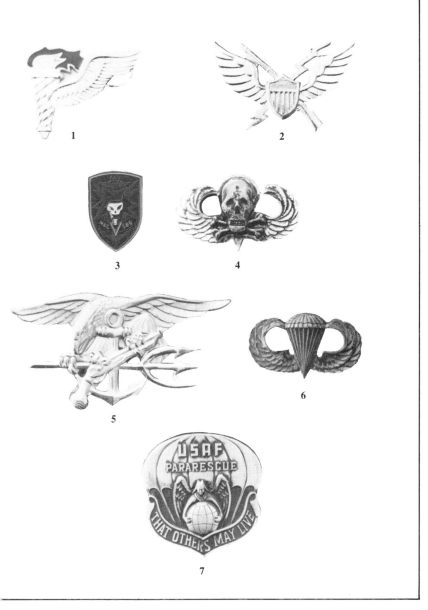

1

2

3   4

5   6

7

hfinder badge. Gold winged torch with white and
me. M; US.
assault badge worn by 11th Air Assault Div which
e 1st Air Cav in Vietnam. M; US.
er can' MACV/SOG DI. White skull with green
n yellow shell burst, red shield. M; SEA.
CV/SOG unauthorized parachutist's wings (widely

faked and very valuable if authentic). Gold skull and
crossbones on silver wings. M; SEA.
5. Navy Special Warfare (SEAL) badge. Gold for
officers; silver for other ranks. M; US.
6. Basic parachutist's brevet. Silver. M; US.
7. Air Force Pararescue beret badge. Silver. M; US.

8

9

10

11

12

13

14

8. MACV Recondo (Reconnaissance Commando) School 'beer can' DI. Black on white. M; SEA.

9. 82nd ABN DI. White fleur-de-lys with the wings and scroll; all else silver. M; US.

10. 505th Parachute Inf DI. Black winged panther, blue stripes and scroll, white parachute with silver wings on silver shield. M; US.

11. 508th Parachute Inf DI. Red cat, blue shield with wide silver stripes, silver scroll with black letters. M; US.

12. 321st Artillery (1st Battn assigned to 101st ABN Div; 2nd Battn assigned to 82nd ABN Div). Red shield and lettering, gold background. M; US.

13. 17th Cav (elements served with 1st Air Cav Div, 82nd ABN Div, 101st ABN Div and 173rd ABN Brigade). Silver wings on yellow and blue background. M; US.

14. 101st ABN Div DI. Black and white eagle, on blue background, gold scrolls with black letters. M; US.

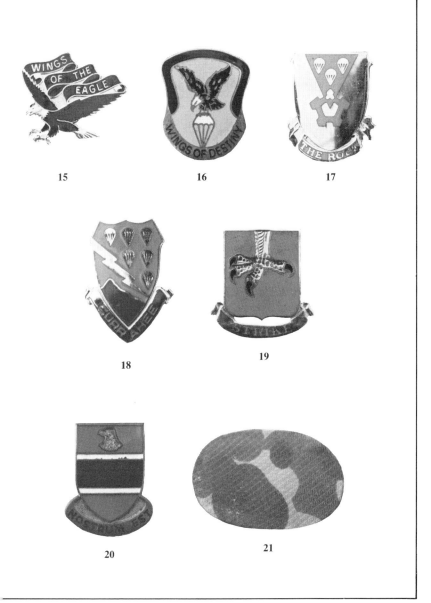

15

16

17

18

19

20

21

1st AVN Battn DI. Black and silver eagle with red
nd silver letters. M; US.
1st AVN Group DI. Black and white eagle with
tail, white parachute with gold detail on blue
und with black border, gold scroll with black
M; US.
3rd Parachute Inf DI. Blue triangle, fortress and
 background silver. M; US.
5th Parachute Inf DI. Silver parachutes and
g bolts, on blue background with green

mountain, silver scroll with black letters. M; US.
19. 502nd Parachute Inf DI. Gold talon with black
claws on blue background, black letters on gold scroll.
M; US.
20. 326th Engineer Battn (assigned to 101st ABN Div)
DI. Gold eagle's head on shield divided blue, white, red,
white, blue; gold scroll with block letters. M; US.
21. Oval reportedly worn by very early Special Forces'
advisors in Laos. Camouflage colors.

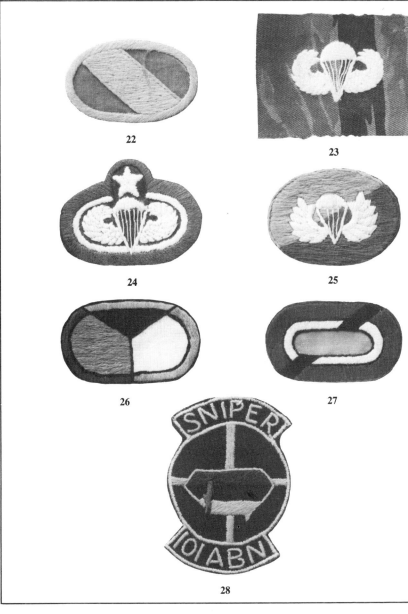

22
23
24
25
26
27
28

22. Special Forces parachute oval. Gold border and band, teal blue background. HM; SEA.

23. Basic parachutist's wings on Tiger-striped material. It should be noted that 'subdued' parachutist's wings were made in black and white in Vietnam on various types of material. Quite often utilities would be custom tailored with the wings and other insignia sewn in. HM; SEA.

24. Oval for the 187th Parachute Inf in Vietnam with senior parachutist's wings sewn in. White wings and ·star, red centre, white inner border, blue outer border. HM; SEA.

25. Oval for the 4th/68th Armor with basic parach wings sewn in. White wings on yellow and green background. HM; SEA.

26. Oval for the 18th Psy Ops Battn. Outer border yellow, red, blue; centre block grey, white. HM; S

27. Oval for the Support units of the 1st Air Cav. outer border, white inner border, yellow centre, b band. HM; SEA.

28. Unauthorized cloth insignia for the 101st AB snipers. Black disc with black tabs, yellow crossb borders, red lettering, central motif black, outline gold, with red detail. HM; SEA.

29   **30**

31

uthorized cloth insignia for the 173rd ABN
snipers; note that a rifle replaces the sword
found on this insignia. White wing with blue
ed rifle, white letters, blue shield and tab with
rders. HM; SEA.
uthorized 82nd ABN Div sniper cloth insignia.

Black rifle, white 'A's in a blue disc with white border,
red background, 'Airborne' white on blue tab, 'Sniper' is
black. HM; SEA.
31. Unauthorized cloth insignia worn by airborne
elements of the 1st Air Cav. Black, yellow and gold. HM;
SEA.

32 **33**

34 **35**

32. Reportedly this locally-made cloth insignia was for elements of the 11th Air Assault Div which served in Vietnam prior to that unit's conversion to the 1st Air Cav. Whether it is authentic is open to some question, but in any case it was unauthorized. White wings, disc border and number, red disc and blue shield. HM; SEA.
33. Subdued 1st Air Cav cloth insignia made in

Vietnam. Black on olive drab. MM; SEA.
34. Cloth insignia for the long range recon patrol of the 1st Air Cav. Black horse, band and borders ground yellow/gold. HM; SEA.
35. Cloth insignia for the recon elements of the 1st Air Cav. (Same colors as 34). HM; SEA.

36

37

38

39

st ABN Div Recondo cloth insignia. White
ad with black border, 'I's in white, 'O' in black,
b border. HM; SEA.

st ABN Div shoulder sleeve insignia. White
nead with yellow beak and black eye, black
ith black tab and yellow letters. HM; SEA.

uthorized 101st ABN Div cloth insignia with

VIETNAM replacing AIRBORNE. (Same colors as 37).
HM; SEA.

39. Reportedly (though open to some question of
authenticity) a locally-made, unauthorized cloth
insignia for elements of the 101st ABN Div. White eagle
with yellow beak on black background. HM; SEA.

40. Cloth insignia for LRRP elements of the 101st ABN Div. White skull, parachute and wings, black background, all other borders, letters, and detail in yellow. HM; SEA.

41. Reportedly (though perhaps not authentic) locally-made, unauthorized insignia for the 101st ABN Div's 'Tiger Scouts'. Tiger Scouts would probably have included VC defectors and other locally-raised irregulars; 'Sat Cong' means 'Kill VC'; 'Bang Chet' means 'Shoot to Kill'; and 'Ho Kick' means 'Tiger Recon'. Small insignia with gold tiger and black detail, letters and numbers black, on blue shield with black border. HM; SEA.

42. Cloth insignia for the 3rd Brigade, 101st A[B] Recon School. Note that instead of ABN the ins[ignia] has AVN. White '3' on white, blue, red, white d[... on] black border, gold letters and numbers. HM; SE[A].

43. Insignia for Battery A, 377th Artillery (AVN) 101st ABN Div. HM; SEA.

44. Unauthorized insignia for elements of the 3rd Brigade, 82nd ABN Div in Vietnam. White para[chute] and lightning bolts with blue detail, figure with [...] legs and arms, black boots and gloves, black le[... on] orange background with black outline. HM; SE[A].

45

46

47

48

49

th insignia for the 505th Parachute Inf. Black
r with red mouth, red parachutes, blue bands
rder on grey background, black numbers. HM;

ignia for the 74th Inf, Long Range Patrol
t of the 173rd ABN Brigade, 'Du Ho Chi Min'
'Screw Ho Chi Minh'. HM; SEA.
ignia for elements of the 502nd ABN Inf. White

bat with black detail, white parachute with black detail,
red, white and blue disc pierced by red and black arrow,
letters and numbers in blue. HM; SEA.
48. Insignia for the 3rd Battn, 506th ABN Inf. Green
snake, white skull, black trident, yellow flames, black
letters, green wreaths on white oval with black border.
HM; SEA.
49. Insignia of the Black Tiger Commandos. HM; SEA.

50

51

52

53

50. Insignia for 1st Battn, 52nd Inf, 198th Inf Brigade, the Long Range Patrol unit for the brigade. White skull, black wings with white detail, red background with black letters. HM; SEA.

51. Beret flash for the 75th Inf (Rangers). Shield with two green and two blue quarters, white and yellow star and sun, red lightning bolt, yellow border. HM; SEA.

52. Insignia for unknown airborne unit. Yellow hea red, white and blue parachute with black border. H SEA.

53. Shoulder sleeve insignia for the 173rd ABN Brigade. Red sword on blue shield with white bord and lettering. HM; SEA.

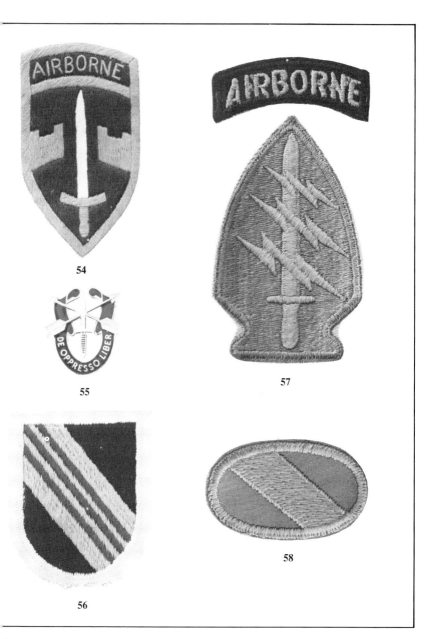

54. for airborne personnel assigned to MACV. Red ~nd tab, yellow letters and border, white sword ~ow handle, yellow fortress. HM; SEA.

55. ~cial Forces crest. Silver arrows, dagger and ~lack scroll. M; US.

56. Special Forces Group (ABN) beret flash. Gold ~th red stripes on black shield with white border.
~.

57. Special Forces shoulder sleeve insignia. Gold sword and lightning bolts, blue background, shaped as arrowhead. MM; US.

58. Special Forces parachute oval. Gold band and border on teal blue background. MM; US.

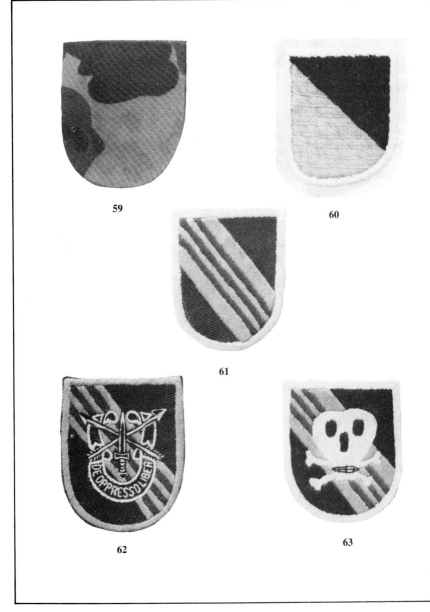

59. Beret flash worn by very early Special Forces advisors in Laos. Camouflage material.

60. Hand-embroidered and quilted 1st Special Forces Group beret flash worn by Special Forces advisors in Vietnam between 1961 and 1963. Black and yellow with white border. HM; SEA.

61. 5th Special Forces Group beret flash. Yellow band with red stripes, black shield with white border. H[ ] SEA.

62. 5th Special Forces Group beret flash with Spe[ ] Forces crest sewn in. As 61 with black and white Special Forces crest sewn in. HM; SEA.

63. 5th Special Forces Group Bright Light Team [ ] flash. As 61 with white skull and crossbones. HM

64

66

65

VIET-NAM
PARACHUTE CLUB NHAY DU

67

Special Forces Group beret flash with rank
sewn in. As 61 with white motif. HM; SEA.
authorized 5th Special Forces Group shoulder
insignia. White skull and crossbones on black
with red border. HM; SEA.
CV/SOG cloth insignia. White skull with green

beret on a black shell burst with yellow border, red
shield and black scroll. HM; SEA.
67. Insignia for the Vietnam Parachute Club. Yellow
freefallers with white detail, white stars, black lettering,
red and white stripes, on white shield with black border.
HM; SEA.

68

69

70

68. Cloth 5th Special Forces Group Command and Control pocket insignia. White helicopter and Army pilot's wings on a white bordered black background with yellow bands and red stripes. HM; SEA.

69. Task Force 1 Advisory Element Communications Section; CCN indicates assignment to Command and Control North. White skull with green beret on a bl arrowhead, yellow lightning flashes and lettering. SEA.

70. CCC cloth insignia. US flag background surrou by a wide blue and narrow yellow border, white sku wings, yellow arrows, black crest, green hat. HM; S

71

72

73

insignia for CCN; note that the shell burst was
sed on MACV/SOG insignia. White skull with
e sockets and nose cavity, green beret, red
black, grey, yellow and red shell burst. CCN in
black scroll. HM; SEA.
Field Training Command pocket insignia.

White skull, green beret, black, yellow and red shell
burst, black scroll. HM; SEA.
73. Mobile Launch Team 2 pocket insignia. White skull
with green beret, eye sockets and nose black, black,
yellow and red shell burst, yellow letters on black scroll.
HM; SEA.

74. Cloth insignia for Forward Operations Base 2. White skull with yellow border, light-blue nose and eye cavities, green beret, black and red shell burst on black background. HM; SEA.

75. Insignia for Mobile Launch Team 2. White skull with green beret, black eye sockets, nose and mouth, red blood on black and gold shell burst, black scroll with yellow letters and border. HM; SEA.

76. Cloth insignia for CCC. White skull with red e red blood from mouth, green beret, black and lig crossed rifles, gold and black shell burst on blue with red border. HM; SEA.

77. Cloth insignia and scroll for Detachment A30 Mobile Guerrilla. Red star and yellow lightning bc black arrowhead with yellow border, black scroll w yellow border. HM; SEA.

78

79

81

80

h insignia for Detachment A-405. White
te, yellow tiger with red eyes and black detail,
ning flash on parachute, green disc with white
etters. HM; SEA.
h insignia for Forward Operations Base 4.
in flag on black staff, brown snake with red
white eyes, black eyeballs, on a yellow disc with
es and black border, black letters and numbers.
A.
n insignia RT Adder. White skull with dark brown
rled around it, impaled on grey knife held by
ored hand, black shield with green border, black

scroll with red letters and green border. MM; SEA.
81. Cloth insignia RT Alabama. (Note the spacing
between the letters in Alabama; I believe that this
insignia has been faked with the letters written together;
however, since many of the RT insignia were made at
different times in different tailor shops it is possible,
even probable, that authentic examples exist with
Alabama written both ways.) White skull with green
beret, black eyes, nose and mouth, grey wings, yellow
tabs with black borders and lettering, black, red and
yellow shell burst, on white rectangle with yellow
border. HM; SEA.

82

83

84

85

82. Cloth insignia RT Alabama. (Note that this is a completely different version of the insignia shown in 81. US Special Forces personnel assigned to RTs were rotated in and out of country frequently, which resulted in new insignia being made up for incoming personnel. As a result many variations exist.) White skull with green beret and black detail, red blood on a black and yellow shell burst, white disc with a red border, red saltire, and green omega sign, CCC in yellow and other lettering blue, white disc with red border. HM; SEA.

83. Cloth insignia for RT Anaconda. (Note that 'snake' recon teams were normally assigned to CCN, while 'state' recon teams were normally assigned to CCC. This

rule is not 100% valid, as exceptions exist. Team allocated to 'snake' and 'state' according to their particular names.) White skull with black eyes, n mouth, black parachute, green beret and green s red eye and tongue of snake, black shield with re letters. HM; SEA.

84. Cloth insignia RT Anaconda. White skull, gre beret, brown snake, yellow disc with black border. I

85. Cloth insignia RT Arizona; 'Watches' probabl to the trail watching or other intelligence gatheri activities of the RTs. White skull in black and red red, yellow, orange, green and black dragon on a rectangle with white border, black letters. HM; S

86

88

87

89

90

insignia RT Arkansas; 'Loi Long' means
ᴈ Dragon' while the Chinese characters mean
ᴈ Dragon' and 'Lightning Ghost Dragon'; on the
y mean 'Recon'. White skull with green wreath,
ᴈon, lightning flash and letters in yellow, blue
ᴈcroll with black border. HM; SEA.
insignia RT Colorado. Grey skull with black
t and mouth with white teeth, white letters,
ᴈld with red border. HM; SEA.
insignia for RT Connecticut; note that 'Epul
tands for 'Montagnard', the hill people who
the indigenous portion of the team. White

skull, green snake, yellow lightning flashes, brown bird,
red lettering on black shield with white outline. HM;
SEA.
89. Cloth insignia RT Colorado – a variation of 87.
White winged skull and rifle, red eye sockets and black
nose, red blood on forehead and mouth, black shield
with red border, 'Airborne' in black, 'Colorado' and 'RT'
in red. HM; SEA.
90. Cloth insignia RT California. White bird, parachute
risers, olive drab parachute, blue disc and red shield
with yellow borders. HM; SEA.

91. Cloth insignia RT Delaware. White skull with green beret, black crossed knife and rifle, lettering and border in orange on white shield. HM; SEA.

92. Cloth insignia RT Diamondback. White skull with green beret, eyes, nose and mouth in grey, green snake, white lettering, yellow shell burst and red disc with black borders. HM; SEA.

93. Cloth insignia RT Florida, very roughly made by

hand; note that the alligator has a VC in its mout[h]. White skull with green beret, green alligator, whi[te] sword on yellow disc with black lettering. HM; S[EA].

94. Cloth insignia RT Fork; note that the shell bu[rst] death's head in green beret theme common in m[any] insignia. White skull with green beret, red eye so[cket,] nose cavity and black mouth, yellow lettering on [...] and yellow shell bursts. MM; SEA.

95

96

97

98

Cloth insignia RT Georgia; the Confederate flag is appropriate to Georgia's southern location, while the comment on the arc is self-evident. Black rifle with white detail, on a confederate flag with a white border, blue tab with white border and letters. HM; SEA.
Cloth insignia RT Hunter. White skull, arm and white blade, brown snake with white stripe on a black shield with green border. MM; SEA.

97. Cloth insignia RT Idaho (a HALO team). Grey lion and yellow 'V', red lettering on a black shield. HM; SEA.
98. Cloth insignia RT Indiana; note this is one of the more crudely sewn RT patches. Red and brown scorpion, green beret pierced by a white knife with black hilt, black letters on a sky blue shield with red tab. HM; SEA.

99

100

101

99. Cloth insignia RT Intruder. White winged skull, knives have grey blades stained with blood, brown hilts, white lettering, yellow band with red stripes on black background. HM; SEA.
100. Cloth insignia RT Iowa. Yellow and black eagle clutching a green snake on a blue triangle with white border and white letters. HM; SEA.

101. Cloth insignia RT Kansas; 'We kill for peace' always been one of my favorite slogans on RT insig White parachute and skull with black wings, a red flamed sun and a yellow cross on a yellow band wi stripes, white and yellow letters on sky blue shield black border. HM; SEA.

102

103

104

th insignia RT Kentucky; note that this is one of st of the hand-embroidered RT insignia. Note the inclusion of the chess piece conjures up team's warlike nature and the origin of its name famous for breeding thoroughbreds. White ce and brown rifle on a US flag and black shield low border, yellow letters with blue scroll. HM;

103. Cloth variation RT Kentucky. Light-blue parachute and red Montagnard cross bow on black background with red border. White lettering. HM; SEA.
104. Cloth insignia RT Louisiana. Yellow head with black hair, red eyes, black tab with gold letters, yellow shell burst with red border, black letters. HM; SEA.

105

106

107

108

105. Cloth insignia RT Maine. Red shell burst with green and orange borders, parachute details outlined in white, CCC is orange, other lettering white, yellow star, white shield with green border. HM; SEA.

106. Cloth insignia RT Mississippi. Light gold eagle clutching yellow tiger, brown, red, black and white detailing, lettering in red on a black shield with red borders. HM; SEA.

107. Cloth insignia RT Mike FAC; beret flash is a Khymer flash. White skull with green beret and black detail on a yellow disc with red border, black scroll with yellow letters. HM; SEA.

108. White skull and crossbones with a green snake, black details and lettering on yellow disc with red border. HM; SEA.

109

110

111

112

th insignia RT Montana. White skull with black
d yellow tiger, black detail on red disc with
der, black scroll with red letters. HM; SEA.
th insignia RT Moccasin; note this is one of the
active of the RT patches because of the
g combination of colors and the detailing.
ull with green beret, red eye socket and black
own knife hilt and purple blade, green snake

with red detail, red lettering and dark-blue shield with
black border. MM; SEA.
111. Cloth insignia RT Oregon (note RT Ohio's insignia
was quite similar). White skull with black outlining on
white shield. HM; SEA.
112. Cloth insignia RT Pennsylvania. Yellow bat with
black outlining on yellow shield with black outlining,
details and lettering. HM; SEA.

113

114

115

116

113. Cloth insignia RT Python. HM; SEA.
114. Cloth insignia RT Puerto Rico. White skull with black outlining and detail, black and white border and white lettering on olive drab shield. MM; SEA.
115. Cloth insignia RT Rhode Island. White bird grasping a green and white snake with red eye and

tongue, black bow and arrow, red lettering on a shield with blue border. HM; SEA.
116. Cloth insignia RT Spike. White skull and crossbones pierced by yellow spike, red and bla detailing, yellow lettering on black disc with red HM; SEA.

117

118

119

120

7. Cloth insignia RT Tarantula. HM; SEA.
8. Cloth insignia RT Weather. White skull with black ail and red blood drops, green beret, yellow lightning h, grey cloud, brown mountains, green foreground, a blue shield. Brown and green letters. HM; SEA.
9. Detachment B-56 Project Sigma insignia; road-ners were indigenous personnel who dressed up as and operated along infiltration routes into South

Vietnam. Black bird with grey detail, red eye, gold beak, red, blue and gold VC flag, yellow lightning flashes, gold lettering on olive drab disc with black border. MM; SEA.
120. Cloth insignia 'D' Company, CCC Exploitation Force insignia. Two-tone brown bird grasping a black axe and green snake on light-blue triangle with white border, black letters, yellow 'Airborne'. HM; SEA.

121

123

122

124

121. Cloth insignia CCC RT; often known as 'The Hulk', the figure on this insignia is of interest. Yellow 'Hulk' with black features, yellow lips, violet eyeballs, black and red pants, red lettering on blue shield with yellow border. HM; SEA.

122. Cloth insignia RT West Virginia; in hand-made and machine-sewn versions, one of the most garish and interesting of the RT insignia. Chinese characters to the left of the head say 'Kill VC'. White skull and lightning flashes, white knife with bloody blade. Chinese characters are red, blue flame on a green disc with gold border, yellow tab with black border, 'CCC' in gold, 'RT West Virginia' in black. MM; SEA.

123. Cloth insignia US Air Force personnel suppo the Son Tay Raid. White mushroom with orange sp a black disc with white scroll with black border anc lettering. HM; SEA.

124. Cloth insignia for those taking part in the Sor Raid; note that insignia normally encountered will stars in the space beneath the arc. Although the a has some reason to believe the insignia illustrated authentic, it should be noted that this is one of the widely faked of Vietnam insignia. Yellow prison to red yard, white arrow and flash, black shield with r white and blue borders, white tab and scroll with g borders, black lettering. HM; SEA.

125

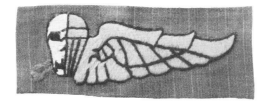

126

127

rc on olive drab for the USMC 1st Recon Battn.
n olive drab. MM; SEA.

SMC Recon Parachutist's wings. White skull and
ngs on camouflage. HM; SEA.

127. Larger variation of USMC Recon parachutist's
wings on Tiger Stripes camouflage material. Same
coloring as 126. HM; SEA.

128 129 130 131

128. Cloth insignia USMC 1st Recon Battn. White skull and crossbones with red '1', white stars, blue diamond, red scroll, yellow letters. HM; SEA.

129. Cloth insignia USMC 2nd Recon Battn. White skull with yellow flame, both detailed in black, black oars, red background with black border, white letters. HM; SEA.

130. Cloth insignia 1st USMC Guerrillas. Grey snake, grey knife blades with brown hilts, white scroll with lettering and border, '1st' in red, other lettering yellow on black background. HM; SEA.

131. USMC parachutist's insignia. Parachute and wings outlined in black on white background, black boots and green and brown camouflaged helmet. HM; SEA.

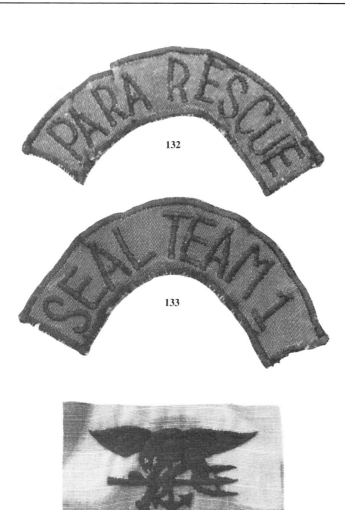

132

133

134

c for USAF Pararescue men. Black on olive
M; SEA.

c for US Navy SEAL Team. Black on olive drab.
.A.

134. US Navy SEAL Special Warfare insignia in black
embroidery on camouflage cloth. HM; SEA.

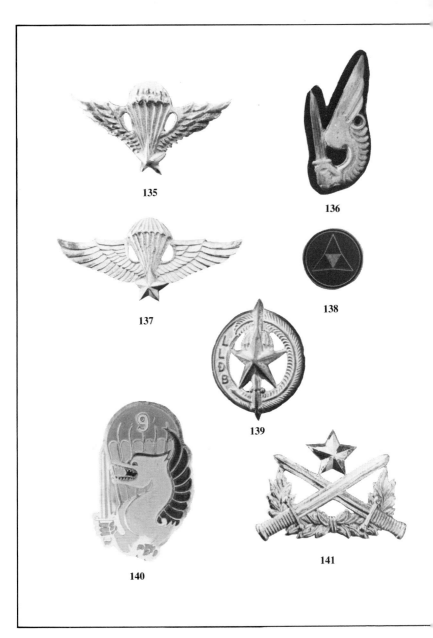

135. Vietnamese basic parachutist's brevet in silver. M; SEA.

136. Vietnamese Jump Status badge in metal on black cloth backing. (Note that a Jump Status badge is worn by those actually assigned to parachute units.) Gold winged hand, silver knife. M; SEA.

137. LLDB parachutist's brevet in metal. Note that insignias 135, 136, 137 are still being made in USA for those personnel qualified to wear them, but the collector should strive for items made in country such as those illustrated here. M; SEA.

138. Beer can DI for the Joint Observation Battn, a fore-

runner of the LLDB. Green caltrap on red disc. M; SEA.

139. Pocket badge worn by early members of the LLDB. Silver. M; SEA.

140. Beer can DI for the 9th ARVN Parachute Ba . Parachute on grey background, blue beast with si detail, red tongue and wing, silver sword, red num M; SEA.

141. Vietnamese Ranger (Biet Dong Quan) breas badge. As with metal para brevets this badge is s produced in the USA, but the collector should att to acquire one made in country. Knife blades silve remainder gold. M; US.

142

143

144

145

146

147

VN basic parachutist's wing. White wing and
e, gold star, black background. SW; SEA.
odued ARVN para wing. Black on olive drab
M; SEA.
VN master para wing. White wing and
e with yellow star and palm in black. SW; SEA.
nd-embroidered ARVN para artillery battn wing.
d white parachute, red wings, yellow shield,

yellow star, black crossed cannons, camouflage background. HM; SEA.
146. ARVN basic para instructor wing. Gold wings and
parachute, yellow and red rings, black background. SW;
SEA.
147. ARVN basic para wing on cloth. White wings on
parachute with gold star on black background. HM;
SEA.

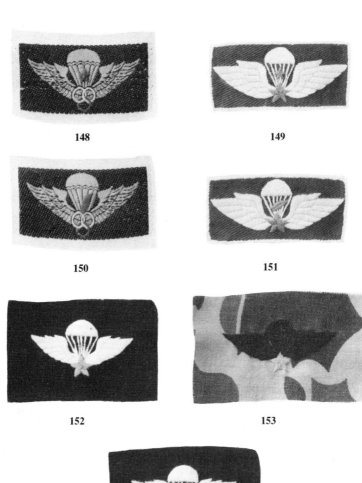

148

149

150

151

152

153

154

148. ARVN senior para instructor wing. Gold wing and parachute, yellow and red wings, red star on black background. SW; SEA.
149. ARVN senior para wing on cloth. White parachute and wings with gold stars on black background. HM; SEA.
150. ARVN master para instructor wing. Gold wings and parachute with yellow and red rings on black background. SW; SEA.
151. ARVN master para wing on cloth. White parachute

and wings with gold leaf and star on black backg
HM; SEA.
152. ARVN basic para wing (variation). White w
parachute with gold star on black background. H
153. ARVN basic para wing (variation). Black wi
parachute with gold star on camouflage backgrou
HM; SEA.
154. ARVN senior para wing (variation). White w
parachute with gold stars on black background.
SEA.

155

156

157

158

159

160

RVN senior para wing (variation). Black wing and
ute with gold stars on camouflage background.
EA.

RVN master para wing (variation). White wing
rachute with gold star and leaf on black
ound. HM; SEA.

RVN master para wing (variation). Black wing
rachute with gold star and leaf on camouflage
ound. HM; SEA.

158. ARVN basic para instructor wing, cloth (variation).
White winged parachute with yellow and red wings on
olive drab background. HM; SEA.
159. ARVN cloth para rigger wing. White wings and
parachute with black outlining and lettering on
camouflage. HM; SEA.
160. ARVN basic para instructor. Gold wing and
parachute with red and yellow rings on camouflage
background. HM; SEA.

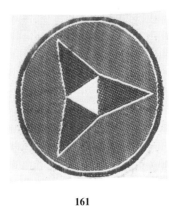

161

162

163

164

161. Joint Observation Battn. Green caltrap with white border and center, on red disc with black border. SW; SEA.

162. 77th ARVN Special Forces Battn. As 161 but with white numbers. SW; SEA.

163. 606th ARVN Special Forces Battn. As 162. SEA.

164. 660th Special Forces Battn. As 162. SW; S

165

166

167

168

ᴏth insignia ARVN ABN/Ranger (Special
'Luc Luong Dac Biet' means 'Vietnamese
Forces'. White parachute with white lines and
tail, white Tony the Tiger with black and yellow
green and black eyes, orange tongue on olive
ᴋground. HM; SEA.
st ARVN Special Forces Battn. As 162. SW;

167. ARVN 77th Special Forces Battn. Black
parachute, yellow map of Vietnam, white lightning
flash, white wings, red star, red lettering on a green
background. SW; SEA.
168. Dong Tre Mobile Guerrilla Force insignia (note
similarity to ARVN Special Forces insignia). Yellow tiger
with black stripes, white lettering and lightning flashes
on a green shield. SW; SEA.

169

170

171

172

169. Subdued ARVN Special Forces insignia. Black on olive drab. SW; SEA.

170. ARVN Special Forces insignia (variation). Yellow tiger with black detail, 3 white stars and tails on green shield. SW; SEA.

171. ARVN Special Forces insignia (variation). A SW; SEA.

172. Task Force 1 (CCN) 'Chien Doan 1 Xung Kic means 'Task Force 1 Strike Force'. White skull, v lightning flashes, yellow and red map of Vietnam letters on a red disc. HM; SEA.

173

174

175

MIKE Force, III Corps. White on black. P;

; the Chinese characters at the bottom of the
tand for 'Recon'. Yellow skull with green beret
knife, yellow lightning flash on black back-

ground with white border. HM; SEA.
175. ARVN 81st Special Forces Group, which later
became a battalion. Red falcon, white flashes, white
parachute, black detail, white circle, yellow number,
black triangle with yellow border. SW; SEA.

176

177

178

179

176. 5th Mobile Strike Force Command (MIKE Forces) were airborne qualified, US Special Forces trained indigenous reaction forces. Yellow lightning flashes, on a blue shield, white knife, black border, black tab with gold 'Airborne'. SW; SEA.

177. ARVN Special Forces Liaison Office insignia. Grey and white tiger with red eyes and mouth, black wing, sky blue mountains, yellow lightning flash, white parachute, red disc with yellow border. P; SEA.

178. C-2 MIKE Force, II Corps. White knife, red bow, yellow lightning flashes, black double tab w yellow lettering on blue shield with yellow border SEA.

179. ARVN Special Forces Technical Directorat parachute and dragon, yellow parachute, yellow on a red shield with white border. SW; SEA.

180

181

182

183

...g Security Forces Platoon (Phu Dinh). White
... P; SEA.

...nown Vietnamese Special Forces insignia.
...ll and crossbones on red shield with yellow
...d lettering. P; SEA.

... MIKE Force, IV Corps 'Don-Vi Tham-Sat'
...econ Unit'. Blue bat with green wings, white

skull with black detail superimposed, 3 red bands,
black lettering on yellow tab, yellow shield with black
border. P; SEA.

183. Unknown ARVN Special Forces insignia 'Quyet-
Tu' means 'Ready to Die'. White skull and crossbones,
red lettering on black shield with white border. P; SEA.

184

185

186

187

184. Buon Sar Pa Mobile Guerrilla Force insignia. White bow and arrow and knife, yellow tiger's head, red lettering and 3 red stripes, green shield. SW; SEA.

185. E Pul Blar Wang Mobile Guerrilla Force insignia. (Note that the bow normally indicates Montagnard indigenous troops since it is their traditional weapon.) As 184. SW; SEA.

186. Mobile Strike Forces pocket insignia. Black c olive drab. HM; SEA.

187. Duc Lap CIDG insignia. Black knife with whit centre, yellow handle with red detail, black bow an arrow with yellow feather, black lettering on red sh with wide yellow border and 3 red stripes. SW; SEA

189

188

190

191

192

bile Strike Force insignia. Black bat with white
crossbones, 3 red stripes, white stars, red
on yellow disc with black border. P; SEA.
bile Strike Force insignia. Black bat with white
red curved bars, black lettering on red disc with
rder. P; SEA.
bile Strike Force insignia. Black bat with white

skull, 3 red stars on green shield with black border, red
lettering. P; SEA.
191. 5th MIKE Force Command. Black parachute,
yellow tiger, white, black and yellow detail on green
shield. SW; SEA.
192. Cloth insignia 5th MIKE Force Command. As 191.
P; SEA.

193

194

195

196

193. Camp Strike Force. (Note a Strike Force is now a full-time paid unit as opposed to militia.) Gold and black tiger on green background. P; SEA.

194. C-1 MIKE Force, I Corps. As 191. P; SEA.

195. Mobile Strike Force insignia; 'Sat Cong' means 'Kill Communists' and 'Bao Ve Que Huong' means 'Defend the Country'. White parachute with black ribs

and risers, 2 yellow flames, yellow tiger with black detail, green tab and scroll with black letters, red shield. P; SEA.

196. Buon Mi Ga Mobile Guerrilla Force insignia Yellow tiger with black detail, yellow band with 3 stripes, yellow tab with red lettering, green shield SEA.

197

198

199

200

201

202

tnamese Ranger tab. Red with black lettering
er. SW; SEA.
tnamese Ranger Recon tab. P; SEA.
tnamese Ranger tab (variation). Black letters
er on yellow background. P; SEA.
ARVN Ranger Group, 30th Battn insignia.
pointed star, black panther's head with red

details, white whiskers and fangs on yellow shield
bordered in black, maroon tab with red and white
letters. SW; SEA.
201. Small Vietnamese Ranger insignia. SW; SEA.
202. Subdued ARVN Ranger insignia. Black on olive
drab. SW; SEA.

203

204

205

206

203. ARVN Ranger insignia. SW; SEA.
204. 1st Div Strike Company insignia. White parachute, black panther outlined in white, white star, red shield. P; SEA.
205. 1st Div Strike Company insignia (variation). Black panther's head with red mouth and green eyes, black

letters, red triangle with black base. P; SEA.
206. 1st Div Strike Company insignia (variation). panther with red mouth and green eyes, white d outline, black letters with white borders on red d bordered in black. P; SEA.

207

208

209

210

211

212

211. Cloth Bien Hoa Province PRU. Brown tiger's head, red and yellow eyes, red tongue, white fangs, yellow and black whiskers, white lettering in red disc. P; SEA.

212. Cloth Kien Giang Province PRU. Black and yellow tiger, black and white eye, red tongue, white fangs, black lettering, white disc with black border. P; SEA.

213

215

216

214

217

oth Binh Tuy Province PRU. White skull and
nes, white lettering, red outline to mouth, black
P; SEA.

oth Binh Thuan Province PRU. White winged
with black detail, yellow stars and lettering on
hield with black borders. P; SEA.

215. ARVN LRRP tab. Black tab with red border and
yellow lettering. MM; SEA.
216. ARVN para beret badge. Gold on red. B; SEA.
217. ARVN ABN Brigade SSI. White parachute, green
bird on maroon with white border. SW; SEA.

218

219

220

221

222

218. ARVN ABN Div SSI. Dark-blue parachute, with black bird with yellow beak and talons, white disc with yellow border on a red square with white border. SW; SEA.

219. ARVN 1st Para Battn DI. White parachute, green dragon with white detail, 2 red flames, yellow and red winged bomb. SW; SEA.

220. ARVN 2nd Para Battn DI. White parachute and winged sword, with a red disc and yellow dragon, and sword detailed in blue. SW; SEA.

221. ARVN 3rd Para Battn DI. White parachute golden winged animal, black detail, red tongue, number. SW; SEA.

222. ARVN 5th Para Battn DI. White bird with g detail, sword and parachute in white with blue d red disc, red number, blue lettering. SW; SEA.

223

224

225

226

227

RVN 6th Para Battn DI. White parachute, gold
s, yellow animal heads with red mouths, yellow
r, black lettering. Note that background colors of
e insignia normally vary by battalion or company
y be green, purple, blue, yellow, orange, red, or
. SW; SEA.
RVN 7th Para Battn DI. White parachute canopy
ey border and blue detail, yellow winged dragon
ue detail, blue lettering. SW; SEA.

225. ARVN 8th Para Battn DI. White parachute canopy,
blue winged horse, red detail, red number. SW; SEA.
226. ARVN 9th Para Battn DI. Red and yellow parachute canopy, light-brown lion with red mouth, red
number. SW; SEA.
227. ARVN 11th Para Battn DI. White parachute with
blue background, yellow bird and knives, red shield,
yellow numbers, red lettering. SW; SEA.

228

231

229

232

230

233

228. ARVN 2nd Para Medical Company DI. Yellow shield with dark-blue parachute, red cross, yellow wreath, black bird with green detail. SW; SEA.
229. Cloth ARVN Jump Status Badge. Yellow winged hand holding white knife, on black background. P; SEA.
230. 3rd Medical Company DI. Blue parachute, red cross on blue background, black bird with white detail, yellow wreath, yellow scroll with orange letters. HM; SEA.

231. 1st Medical Company DI. White parachute w red cross, white bird, blue scroll with yellow bord red letters. HM; SEA.
232. ARVN Para Support Battn DI. White parach detail. Yellow bird with black detail, cog, etc., wh with black borders. SW; SEA.
233. Vietnamese Marine Brigade SSI. Yellow glo anchor and eagle with black detail, red star with y map of Vietnam on a black shield. SW; SEA.

234

236

235

237

etnamese 2nd Marine Battn insignia. Blue and
uffalo with red eyes and lips, white lettering on a
ield. P; SEA.
etnamese Marine Div Pocket insignia; 'Danh-Du
' means 'Honour and Country'. Yellow with red
yellow map of Vietnam, yellow lettering on a
sc. P; SEA.
etnamese 1st Marine Battn insignia. Light

brown owl with yellow, black, red and white detailing,
white stars, red'1', white lettering on a black and purple
shield with yellow border. SW; SEA.
237. Vietnamese 3rd Marine Battn insignia. Black sea
wolf with red mouth, black shield and trident, yellow
lettering, black shield with yellow and red disc. SW;
SEA.

238

239

241

240

238. Vietnamese 4th Marine Battn insignia. Black fish with light blue border, black, white and red details, blue lettering, light-blue triangle, red shield, with white outer border and blue border. SW; SEA.

239. Vietnamese 7th Marine Battn insignia. Grey and black tiger with red detail, orange number, grey lettering on green shield with white border. SW; SEA.

240. Vietnamese 5th Marine Battn insignia. White globe with red detail, black dragon with yellow a white detail, red number, black lettering on red ι and blue inner shield. SW; SEA.

241. Vietnamese 8th Marine Battn insignia. Bla with white detail, red eye, yellow map of Vietnan number and letters on green shield with white bc SW; SEA.

242

243

244

245

etnamese 6th Marine Battn insignia. Yellow
with black detail and white border, red '6' and
order, black lettering, green shield with green
nd yellow inner borders. SW; SEA.
3th Vietnamese Navy River Patrol Group (LLDN
es presence of Viet SEALs in the unit). White sea
d '58', black anchor, yellow lettering, on blue
P; SEA.

244. Viet SEAL insignia on camouflage material; to
differentiate units colored thread is used to outline the
tanks and other gear. Colors used are: red, green,
yellow, blue, purple, specifics of which detachments
wore which colors are unknown. Black on camouflage.
HM; SEA.
245. Viet SEAL insignia embroidered (variation). Black
on camouflage. HM; SEA.

SELECT BIBLIOGRAPHY

BRAGG, R. J. and ROY TURNER, *Parachute Badges and Insignia of the World*. Blandford, Poole, 1979.

OURARI, BAUDOUIN, *Badges and Uniforms of the World's Elite Forces*, Volume 1. B&P Military Publications, USA and Brussels, 1984.

SMYTH, CECIL B. Jr, *Army of the Republic of Vietnam Ranger Insignia*. ARV-CAT, Glendale, 1975.

—— *Insignia of the Republic of Vietnam Armed Forces*. Virginia Beach, 1982.

—— *Special Forces in Southeast Asia*. ARV-CAT, Glendale, 1978.

—— *Vietnam: US Army Combat Unit Insignia*. Virginia Beach, 1983.

STANTON, SHELBY L., *Vietnam Order of Battle: US Army and Allied Ground Forces, 1961–73*. US News Books, Washington, D.C., 1984.